A CRACKLING OF THORNS

Volume 54 of the
Yale Series of Younger Poets.
Edited by W. H. Auden
and published on the
Mary Cady Tew Memorial Fund

A Crackling of Thorns

by John Hollander

Foreword by W. H. Auden

New Haven: Yale University Press, 1958

© 1958 by Yale University Press, Inc.
Printed in the United States of America by
the Printing-Office of the Yale University Press.
All rights reserved. This book may not be
reproduced, in whole or in part, in any form
(except by reviewers for the public press),
without written permission from the publishers.
Library of Congress catalog card number: 58–6538.

Most of these poems originally appeared in the following publications:
Hudson Review, The Paris Review, Poetry, Discovery,
New Directions, The Harvard Advocate, Commentary, Quarto, Partisan
Review, Kenyon Review, Audience, The Columbia Review, The New
Republic, The Chicago Review, The Atlantic Monthly, and The Sewanee
Review. "The Bawd's Song" and "The Lady's-Maid's Song" were written
for a production of Etherege's "The Man of Mode," produced at Barnard
College May 1951. Some of the poems also appeared in New Poets of
England and America, an anthology published by Meridian Books.
"A Theory of Waves" and "The Great Bear" originally
appeared in The New Yorker.

for Anne and for Mickey

Foreword

Every poem, be it big or small, simple or complex, is recognizably a world. What we call *the* world we infer to be a world, but no individual can perceive it as such; for each of us it is broken into fragments, some of which he knows quite well, some a little, some not at all, and even of those he knows best he can never truthfully say "I know what it is" but only "I know what it was."

In a poetic world, however, these obstacles to knowledge are eliminated: in a poem there are no strangers—every inhabitant is related to every other and the relationship is known; there are no secrets—a reader may notice something on a second reading which he missed on the first, but it was never concealed; there is no chance—the series of cause and effect is without any hiatus; and there is no time but the present—nothing can grow, die, or change.

There is among poetic worlds, however, an element of physical diversity which is lacking in the worlds, for instance, of painting and music; though the inhabitants of all poetic worlds are made of a verbal substance, this has developed into different linguistic strains which rarely permit of intermarriage. English is a more mongrel tongue than most and, for this reason, is perhaps the least prejudiced against words of another color; but even in English successful assimilation is rare and cannot be hurried.

So far as the practical and political life of the world is concerned, what happened at the Tower of Babel must, no doubt, be regarded as a curse but for poetry I can imagine no greater blessing. Indeed, at a time when so many of the forces making for world unity are so dangerous and disagreeable, the defiantly parochial character of poetry may even have an extra-artistic moral value. One can imagine a future world in which everybody on earth believes the same dogmas, obeys the same authorities, and is nourished on the same diet; but one cannot imagine a world in which Hungarian poetry, let us say, would be indistinguishable from Finnish.

It is just and proper that literary criticism should concern itself primarily with those problems and values which are common to all poetry, the nature of image and metaphor, the boundaries between the poetic and the nonpoetic, etc.; but it should also keep a place for the consideration of that which is peculiar to the poetry of a particular tongue, of those elements in a poem which are a priori untranslatable. Thus, while metaphors are usually, at least in theory, translatable, it is obvious that puns are not.

When Mr. Hollander writes:
>The question was whether to live like trees or towers,
>Evolving from the bare hills like conifers,
>Pretending ignorance of the changes of winter,
>Or standing bare as sorrow in the snow,
>Striped red and green to show one's parentage
>In the colored rocks of the hills he's quarried from.
>Was memory to be the philogeny of towers
>Or the languages of trees? A Past, that honors
>Bright spears and perils held surely to the canter,
>Or a History, with garlands at the brow
>Of verdure and all her silent heritage?
>The branch, or the eternal stone to come?

for all the complexity of this passage, one can imagine a translation of it into another tongue which would be intelligible so long as, in the culture which spoke that tongue, towers, trees, and time had the same kind of significance that they have in our English-speaking culture. But when he writes:

Europe, Europe is over, but they lie here still,
While the wind, increasing,
Sands teeth, sands eyes, sands taste, sands everything.

one cannot imagine any translation which would at once give the overt meaning and recall the line from Jaques' speech. (The operative word in this case reminds me of a line by Humbert Wolfe which I cannot resist quoting. " 'Sugar,' he said, and pointed to the sand.")

Puns are, of course, a minor matter, but the linguistic idiosyncrasy of which they are an extreme case is exhibited in every aspect of poetry that is concerned with forms.

Many of Mr. Hollander's most successful poems are songs or, at least, "words for music perhaps." The song—the lyric is not quite the same thing—is, of all kinds of poetry, the one in which the formal verbal elements play the greatest role and are, indeed, the main source of interest. In the world of the song, one might say, the important relationship between the inhabitants is not any community of concern or action so much as family kinship. The satisfaction I get from reading a poem by Campion, for example, is similar to the satisfaction I get from studying a well worked out genealogical tree. (A wet afternoon could be pleasantly spent developing this analogy. Starting with the notion that masculine rhymes represent brothers, feminine rhymes sisters, refrains identical twins, one could ask what verbal relationship would be equivalent to a second cousin once removed. From there one could go on to consider what discords correspond to marriage within the prohibited degrees, e.g., to marrying one's deceased wife's sister.)

English is a language to which the most natural measured rhythm is accentual iambic; it has many common monosyllables, the metrical value of which depends not upon their intrinsic quantity but upon their position in the line; and it has, relatively, few rhymes, in particular few noncomic feminine rhymes. The criteria, therefore, by which one judges a song writer are firstly, his ability, by the use of equivalence and substitution of feet, to avoid rhythmical monotony without falling into rhythmical anarchy; secondly, his ability to vary the line length within a stanza in a way that sounds natural to what is said; and lastly, his skill in the finding of rhymes which sound neither forced nor cliché and in the placing of them so that the stanza is made an indivisible whole.

To my ear Mr. Hollander passes all these tests with ease.

> Advocate the cause of cloth,
> Though it's absurd;
> And tender a suit against the moth;
> Question him, and watch his sloth
> To speak a word.
> The furry silence that he keeps
> Can be shown to be
> Like the one that creeps
> From quiet Roseblush as she sleeps
> As silent as the moth, but not with me;
> Softly in a bush, but not with me.

The use of masculine rhymes throughout preserves the iambic ground, but the omission of the first syllable in lines one, four, and eleven suggests a trochaic counterpoint; in lines seven and eight there is a felicitous hint of the anapaest, which is, however, kept within bounds since it is possible to scan these lines either as three feet or as two. The lines vary in length from five feet to two, and it will be noticed how Mr. Hollander keeps his stanza together by his placing of the rhymes in relation to this variation; sometimes rhyme and line length coincide, sometimes they run in contrast.

He is particularly skillful in his handling of feminine rhymes. The following two examples show what a difference the placing of such rhymes can make to the whole movement of a stanza.

Save one who, with a pair
Of emeralds at her ear,
 Felt for her shining toys
  And nestled to their nearness,
 Making a tiny noise,
Idolatrous and bald.
 This was unenvying queerness.
The boys were quite enthralled.

———

Living with men has made me
A dialectical cat;
Ergo, I argued that
Her course was to upbraid me:
She refused and she spat
(She claimed no punishment
But held that I'd repent).
 All this was repaid me
When, at the end of the quarrel,
I had her over a barrel.

They also show how, in a song, the thought and emotion, what the words *mean,* are inseparable from the form, the way in which the words move. It is impossible to imagine the one without the other: both are two aspects of a single imaginative act which, like all acts of the imagination, is a marriage of the given to the calculated.

In longer, nonlyrical, discursive poems, the element of conscious calculation is likely to be greater, and greater the danger, therefore, of a form which seems arbitrarily imposed upon the subject matter.

The test in such cases is, I believe, the opposite of what it is in a song. In a song the reader should be immediately aware of the formal structure, but in a discursive poem the latter should be unobtrusive so that he does not perceive it unless he deliberately looks for it.

In several poems Mr. Hollander has set himself the formidable task of constructing a fourteen-line stanza.

> Feeling that it is vaguely undignified
> To win someone else's bet for him by choosing
> The quiet girl in the corner, not refusing
> But simply not preferring the other one;
> Abashed by having it known that we decide
> To save the icing on the chocolate bun
> Until the last, that we prefer to ride
> Next to the window always; more than afraid
> Of knowing that They know what sends us screaming
> Out of the movie; even shocked by the dreaming
> Our friends do about us, we vainly hope
> That certain predictions never can be made,
> That the mind can never spin the Golden Rope
> By which we feel bound, determined, and betrayed.

Beyond noticing that all the lines are five-foot iambic and that there are rhymes, one's attention at first reading is concentrated upon what is being said, and one will never be obliged to see the structure unless one is curious about such matters. But if one investigates one will see that, in its rhyme structure, the stanza divides into two symmetrical halves rhymed abbcaca, the b's being feminine.

To prevent the stanza simply breaking in two Mr. Hollander allows no pause in sense at the end of the seventh line and generally, indeed, allows such pauses only in the middle of lines; thus the main pause comes in the middle of line eleven with subsidiary pauses in the middle of lines three, seven, eight, and ten. Further, there is no full stop until the end of the final line.

If in "The Fear of Trembling" and "The Great Bear," which are also written in fourteen-line stanzas, though differently constructed, the form seems more obtrusive than it ought to be, one of the reasons is that Mr. Hollander runs the sentences on from one stanza to the next so that the choice of fourteen lines seems a bit arbitrary.

In the pleasure he takes in begetting closely knit verbal clans, Mr. Hollander is a traditionalist, but he also shows a desire, characteristic of our own time, for the maximum amount of physical diversity. Like many modern poets, one of the questions he puts to himself is: "How many oddities, dwarfs, giants, albinos and the like can I credibly make my family breed? What variety of costume and haircut can I make socially tolerable?" This search for diversity is apt to breed a family of Bohemian eccentrics; that is to say, it is usually more successful when the poem is intended to be comic or seriocomic.

> I should rather
> Not involve her father,
> Nor did some bumbling fool
> Push her into the pool
>   Without design;
> And we are all far subtler
> Than to accuse The Butler.
>   Waly O how rotten
>   That she was never mine.

In a serious poem there is a greater risk.

>   For then, with the sun upon us, we remember
>   That old prayers were extrapolations, fears
>   Held in the cold were no mere casual guesses . . .

It was sporting of Mr. Hollander to try to get in "extrapolations," but the result, I'm afraid, is a miscarriage.

I suppose Mr. Hollander must be called a "literary" poet in the sense that the inhabitants of his poems know more about poetry, particularly poetry of the seventeenth century, than they know about, say, gardening or cooking; and one has the impression that, on returning from a walk, they could tell one more of what they had worried about than of what they had seen. But, after all, why shouldn't they? Parnassus is a free country. Besides, when the worrier does manage to look at something, he may see what the naturalist would miss.

> No wind we know can stir
> This olive blackness that surrounds us when
> It becomes the boundary of what we know
> By limiting the edge of what we see.
> When sunlight shows several spruces in a row,
> To know the green of a particular tree
>   Means disbelief in darkness; and the lack
>   Of a singular green is what we mean by black.

W. H. Auden

Contents

FOR CERTAIN OTHERS

"For as the crackling of thorns under a pot,

so is the laughter of a fool."

R. Levi b. R. Zeira made this the text of his address . . .
and said: When all other woods are kindled their sound
does not travel far; but when thorns are kindled, their
sound travels far, as though to say, "We too are wood."
Midrash Rabbah, Eccles. 7:6.

For Actors

Icarus before Knossos

FOR DONALD COOK

Winter, in a white rage of urgency,
From what we know of knowledge, serves it poorly,
And the cold, the cold alone, in painful freezing
Dries up so much motion that the course
Of measurement is shriveled to a trace,
The following finger, gliding eye, and ranging
Sense, all stopped, as in an emergency
Of waiting. The sun will start them moving, surely,
When the spring comes, the river bed releasing
New turbulence, the frozen field, its marsh,
And vision, all the fluid processes
Which comprehend embellishment and changing.

But can the sun surely save us? In December
The fixed precision of cold and snow infers
The eventual elegance of thaws and freshets,
But when the frozen sense of measurement
Revives and moves like wild emergent honey,
We cannot accept our winter propositions;
For then, with the sun upon us, we remember
That old prayers were extrapolations, fears
Held in the cold were no mere casual guesses:
There will be no sun this spring. The sun is spent.
Meanwhile the sun's own seasonal miscellany
Proclaims on every page our death's directions.

Thus reasoning, and having thoroughly read
Various journals of my own few seasons,
I turned to that golden annal of the heart:
The Very Rich Hours, the old illuminations
Of love's most famous scenery, and marked

How, through the very Hiems and the Vers,
The prospect held its properties, and bred
Simple disguises for its several versions.
Here, though, a tower and there, a tree imparted
A fearful permanence to those bright distractions
Bound in the book of all my own heart's work,
A passage too continuous to be parsed.

The question was whether to live like trees or towers,
Evolving from the bare hills like conifers,
Pretending ignorance of the changes of winter,
Or standing bare as sorrow in the snow,
Striped red and green to show one's parentage
In the colored rocks of the hills he's quarried from.
Was memory to be the philogeny of towers
Or the languages of trees? A Past, that honors
Bright spears and perils held surely to the canter,
Or a History, with garlands at the brow
Of verdure and all her silent heritage?
The branch, or the eternal stone to come?

No longer being young, I can remember
Many trees, and the effigies of trees,
Tuscany and spruces, bright squares of Venice,
Pale domes, palmettos, and the shocking cactus
Of our own adequate West, the impact of images
Observed on journeys entirely by train;
Not yet being old, I have still time to consider
More journeys taken in a rage, and effigies
Of towers that look like trees, and will surely vanish.
But to put these dialectics into practice
I'll await no ceremonies of future rages,
For trees may be trained to look like towers by then;

Or towers like trees: old images, and awkward,
Explained by the leaveless shapes of cold December

But not without terror for me. I had the fear
That in such architecture was designed
My own undoing: Gray buttresses of branches,
Stones cut like leaves and crossed with mullioned fronds,
And above all, the bells, so rudely quartered,
And above that, an even more cramped chamber
Where you, *maudit sois tu,* carilloneur,
Rang changes out on the bronzed fruit, comprised
Of seasonal intervals, till the bells in bunches
Dropped, crying *Autumn, autumn!* to the winds.

Those syllables rang our death, could we contrive
To prove that towers were founded in the air
For purposes of the bells, or the sorrowful clocks,
Inevitably articulate in the silence
Of structured branches and high, arch espaliers
Of stone. Could we irrevocably commend
Those hours and bells to our attention, love
Might never find the sure escapement there,
Nor lands, lit by versions of the sun we lack,
House our retreating hearts in fiery dalliance,
For in time the goldenmost of shining trees
Emerge in fierce white winter at fall's end.

But as fruit itself must drop, in the rusts of autumn,
It falls to the pealing of the bells to crack
With cold, where the pallid eye of the wintered sun
Governs the runnings of the months, whose fashions
Of careless and phenomenal change subvert
The truest tower or the oldest tree;
But I dared publish, in one agreeable emblem,
The tower and the tree, and turned my back
On lunatic winter's generations
Of marshy flight and white return, its passing,
Seasonal governments of the frightened heart
Which go unpunished in their simony.

3

And I journeyed from the North, and stopped to sit
In this ringed city, in the South of Something,
Hung under the sun by old geometers,
Constructed to maintain a shining commerce
Over the green sea, washing the rocks at its feet.
Set high above the burning cliffs above them,
Birds perch on golden finials, and lit
By an eternal sun, describe in their turning
No differences of wind, but what appears
To serve this silent city as a promise
Left by departing gods as they plunged, reeling,
Under the cold green washes of the ocean.

Upon that promise I turned an augury
That pierced through the binding and reflected sunlight
With the golden and prophetic craft; it read:
There will be no spring in the sun. The months are spent.
December and the others have fled their names
And seasons; the final shining of the sun
Has merged with fragments of the winter's fury
The spring's relenting tempers, and even tunneled
Under the thundering sea, lest there be laid
Submerged, on the structures of its floor, the bent
And rusted relics of those seasonal changes
Which fouled its triumph of redemption.

And upon that prophecy I have turned to journey
Over the wild surge, in a tumbling ship,
Breaking the cloudy spume and following after
Wide bays and curving beaches, while its course
Holds always to the one, quotidian,
High engine of ascendancy, overhead.
The wind trumpets hoarsely through the waves; we turn
Toward the ultimate island, whose first blazing cape
The sun discerns, across the roaring water:
Painted Crete is upon us, and all its shores

4

Show forth, as we cross the last meridian
That marks the land's edge and the water's end,

And where, at the brink of the bay, a ploughman turns
His implement into the hill, not as he would
In the mild agriculture of a pastoral,
But, having wrung the ever-ripening fruit
From out his orchard, urges his devotion
Upon the earth in fury, all unaware
Of my arrival and deliverance.
Is his mute husbandry to be understood
As a rite of love? or as a festival
Of fear for the myth delivered at his feet,
As though, tomorrow, full over the green ocean,
He might behold it, falling from the air?

Orpah Returns to Her People

RUTH 1:14

It is another country, surely,
Whose road, toward the sun
And toward fine bright fields of barley,
Glides behind limes, and is gone.
I'll return to our northern river, sourly
Rained and snowed upon.
Though their grain flourish, I must go
Riverward, to cold and snow.

Ruth is a flushed rose; her new mother
Leans on her like rain.
Her white thighs will support another
Soon in a bale of grain.
But home, beside my father's river
Where I have always lain,
The northern rains will come and go
And leave me with a child of snow.

Ruth will glean for a new master
When the fields are full:
For him she'll reap and flock the faster
Till all their tools are dull.
My man is dead. No other's pasture,
Grain, nor lineaged bull
Can husband me ever. I must go
Back home now, over stones and snow.

Susanna's Song

While bathing, if the sun should fail,
Caused by clouds to darken me,
The water on each shining tile
Will flash up from below the knee
And water me in a good light
—I did not choose to bathe at night—
Unclouded here by any tree.
Under trees a glade is shady
And no place to bathe a lady.

My bath is white with tiles, the grass
Along its edge is very green.
The sun moves, and green shadows pass
Not too near, but I have seen
That shadows are dark, and I must have
Shadows by me while I bathe,
That I may know when I am clean.
The oak and mastic tree are shady
And water is bright that bathes a lady.

There are old men in mastic trees,
Arms in oaks, and hands in the grass;
Their shadows will reach above my knees
And play with the light on me, unless
The clouds go dark and drift too near
And sun and shadows disappear.
But they will stay while I undress
Not far from where the ground is shady,
The right place to bathe a lady.

The Lady's-Maid's Song

When Adam found his rib was gone
 He cursed and sighed and cried and swore
And looked with cold resentment on
 The creature God had used it for.
All love's delights were quickly spent
 And soon his sorrows multiplied:
He learned to blame his discontent
 On something stolen from his side.

And so in every age we find
 Each Jack, destroying every Joan,
Divides and conquers womankind
 In vengeance for his missing bone.
By day he spins out quaint conceits
 With gossip, flattery, and song,
But then at night, between the sheets,
 He wrongs the girl to right the wrong.

Though shoulder, bosom, lip, and knee
 Are praised in every kind of art,
Here is love's true anatomy:
 His rib is gone; he'll have her heart.
So women bear the debt alone
 And live eternally distressed,
For though we throw the dog his bone
 He wants it back with interest.

For *The Man of Mode*

The Bawd's Song

When I began to work, I found
That men were simpler than I'd thought:
Though peaches, pears, and grapes abound,
It's oranges they've always bought.
    Apples are called the fruit of sin,
        Lovers maintain the fig's a treasure,
    But wise men know they must begin
        With oranges for easy pleasure.

All my goods are quickly sold
The minute even one is tried,
For if the rind looks sick and old,
You'll find 'em sweet enough inside.
    For every man whose own sweetheart
        Deals him a wry and bitter measure
    (Although each sweet's a little tart)
        Ripe oranges are easy pleasure.

Call me a bawd and have it done,
Curse me or laugh and roll your eye,
But every night my sweets are gone
For gentlemen will always buy.
    Convenient sweets are what I sell:
        Whether you live in toil or leisure
    To harp in heaven or burn in hell,
        Here's oranges for easy pleasure.

                For *The Man of Mode*

Songs for Glaucon

A HAG AT A CROSSROADS

Ἄλλην δρῦν βαλάνιζε, Μενέσθιον

GREEK ANTHOLOGY

Attack another oak, old woman,
Shake its acorns off.
Like an apple formed in famine
Your old rind is rough;
Your hair is ruined like worn iron,
Your only song, a cough.
Attack another oak, or go
Converse in coughs with a white crow.

My road approached a broad young reed
Before you stopped to look,
She and I might have done the deed
Then bathed in a swift brook.
But looking, you wanted; wanting, stayed;
And staying an hour, you've stuck.
Your breast is dry, your blood runs slow:
Go give suck to some white crow.

The moon might distract me: it is round.
Your face is brown as trout.
My road maintains its way beyond
Cracked shutters on your house.
Last night you knitted, sat and planned,
Then coughed your candle out.
Then fish in a trickle tonight, or go
And set out snares for a white crow.

GLAUCON MUDDLES A LESSON

Republic 6. 509–13.

Winter in a lumbering line
Has crept to a changed season.
The polar limits of his mind,
Formerly fixed and frozen,
Have melted to a new design,
Made of the circle's reason.
Spring is no clear season:
But bending, she and I can sing
Because we have escaped the spring.

Now as December's line of march
Has driven through to summer,
Her body, like a bend of birch,
Grows round, as though a hammer
Had driven, pounded, bled, and parched,
And left her all the warmer,
Sapped for the whole summer
Of winter's chill, whose loss we sing
Now that we have escaped the spring.

From a divided line we learn
Four faculties of knowing;
In brittle winter once they served
To tell me it was snowing.
But she will teach me, in her turn,
To bend the line by throwing
The golden ball of knowing
Up in the air, and then we'll sing
Of how we have escaped the spring.

By the long, dry, despondent lake
Dusted by late fire,
My pipe is bent and newly cracked:
I've pitched it in the mire;
For all the notes have run awreck,
My wind's begun to tire.
What can be done? My pipe is gone
And all the tunes done thereupon.

The girl who answering danced to them
Lies quietly in clover.
The words she sang I cannot name
Nor their new tune discover.
The path along which we have come
Old leaves have rusted over;
And, like the sun, my pipe is gone
With all the tunes done thereupon.

Tomorrow, when the sun comes up,
I can cut me another;
She will hear it, her every step
Falling like a feather.
And when she falls asleep, perhaps
Better for her rather
Not to know that my pipe is gone
And all the tunes done thereupon.

In this thin disc, wrapped in smoke,
Pale Artemis was seen
By Greeks who knew that circles broke
Direction in a line.
My mind is a line; face, breast, and back
Are curved. This disc is a plane.

Now hard Connecticut will rock
My dark departing train
Past steel Bridgeport, wrapped in smoke,
And the moon will wane.
My mind is a moon; below, the track
Runs by where some girl has lain.

She was curved; the flat disc, round:
My road is a line along the ground.

The girl I passed at a late turning
Has merged with the firs,
The river sobs by where she's running,
And hardly a leaf stirs.
The stars are lessons for my learning
And the moon for hers.

Although she carried on her arm
The clothes that she once wore,
Ahead, the line of road is firm,
Behind, a winding blur.
I do not think that I shall turn,
Or look, or follow her.

The Shopkeeper's Madrigal

Love lately done deserves of no redress,
    Nor from fleeing lover
    Shall obtain it ever;
Such honest venture then were profitless:
    Silver at the starting,
    No interest at parting.
  Love's sweet goods, dearly spun and loomed,
  For the mere kissing are consumed,
Leaving the lip their debt in bitterness.

The greater debt falls due when love's ill-made;
    Time will help accrue it
    Nor can he undo it.
Such serious merchants as myself have paid
    Higher costs for loving
    Than love's worth the having.
  Nothing done or changed or spent
  But must be served with increment;
Thus custom and my care shall wed in trade.

Love's fiscal span is marked from spring to spring;
    Loving is to borrow,
    Tonight must pay tomorrow;
Love's spendthrift comes bare to the reckoning.
    Reason's worth a penny
    But he hasn't any,
  Who each night dies without a hearse
  Because the heart's an empty purse.
Then I'll be rich; let lovers beg and sing.

Carmen Ancillae

BURGUNDY C. 1430

Wider than winter
Lying over the river
Or the frosty sky through the window
That stretches forever
Around the white pennants
Above the battlements;
Wider than all I remember
Is the bed in my Lady's chamber.

Whiter than my Lady
Gazing along the river
At the sunny grass where lately
Her liking had led her
Away from the remnants
Of frost on the battlements;
Whiter than was December
Was the bed in my Lady's chamber.

Cold is the basin
I dip into the river
When the morning sun is blazing
Beyond the crisp weather.
    With its cold contents
    I cross the battlements.

    My Lady's bed is colder,
    Almost, than the river.
    When we were younger
    We warmed it together,
    Warmer than the anger
    She showed as she grew older.

Gold shines in the water
I carry from the river.
Gold given a king's daughter
Can only enrich the giver.
       And what of my penance
       Along the battlements?

       What I bring her looks golden:
       Will it avail me ever?
       Today she will be married,
       Clothed in gold like the river.
       I have fetched and carried:
       She will think of it seldom.

Black as the pearl she gave me
To tie among my tresses
Was her face as she bade them save me
Old robes and dresses
As parting presents.
I can see from the battlements
How she stands in a temper
Of tears and rage in her chamber.

Fragments of a Picaresque Romance

Stand by some convenient tree,
Hands full of money,
Convincing every humble bee
You've discovered currency
Slow as gold honey.
If you await their feigned replies:
Buzz buzz buzz, you'll be
        More generally wise
     And you'll know why Roseblush lies
As civilly as bees, but not with me;
Civilly indeed, but not with me.

Advocate the cause of cloth,
Though it's absurd;
And tender a suit against the moth;
Question him, and watch his sloth
To speak a word.
The furry silence that he keeps
Can be shown to be
        Like the one that creeps
     From quiet Roseblush as she sleeps
As silent as the moth, but not with me;
Softly in a bush, but not with me.

When all the wild red things she's worn
Hang like cousins in a closet,
She'll think of one she's bruised and torn
When, though pale, she's tried to lose it.
Once retrieved, she can't refuse it;
Yet she fears its kind return,
Like a dead cousin's winding sheet
She'd gone and lost along the street.
Better let it burn, she said;
Better let it burn.

This warring and benevolence
I will not have; nor would I change her,
For she would offer no defense
And lend her body to a stranger.
"The predication of love's danger
Lies in refusals to deceive";
And I would foxily concur,
And go, and tell no tale of her
To let her learn and grieve in bed,
To let her learn and grieve.

Once, at a word, she reddened so
All pale disdaining now belies her;
But since, her coloring grown slow,
She'd need a rainbow to advise her.
If distance proves me any wiser,
I'll by far the wiser be;
She, wanting of sufficient haste,
Shall as pursuer yet be chased,
While past her soft away I'll tread,
Soft and speedily.

But if her coloring be quick
And pink as skin has never worn it,

I'll wear the red, as Simple Dick:
She'll play as bee, and I'll be hornet;
Night's colored dead, and thus we'll mourn it
Till our coloring is dun.
Then, to redress the sky for night,
We'll wear that coloring to white,
And scratch it to the bone instead,
    And scratch it to the bone.

I, who have affected
Learning and remorse
Never held good manners
Improper out of doors
Until an old man showed me
All that grace abhors
—The boneyard, of course,
To which I'll be elected.

I've always played at knowing
The nature of the weather,
Pitting knowledge and
Despair against each other;
But now they hold dominion
Like kings allied together
    Over wherever
It may or not be snowing.

If I'm undone in London
Who'll love or honor me?
Unless I were to bend and
Demand alms of the sea,
Nor man nor star nor girl's bare arms
Could bear my perfidy;
    My grave would agree
With his bears' arms I've punned on.

The gentler arms of battle
May ring about my head
In celebration that has made
Old cities kneel and wed.
Although imposing Rome was
No virgin, yet she bled;
    And, for an *aubade,*
Morning came with a rattle.

Love's flame is fairly steady,
For love can ill afford
That final bifurcation
That's fired by the sword;
When brands and ashes drop,
Smoke goes up like a bird:
    Raze me, O Lord;
My beard's too long already.

Her epitaph was never read.
Gone was the stone above her head,
Robbed by a needy sculptor
Who never could have helped her,
Nor had her maidenhead
Before she was dead
   At twenty-nine.
Before she was married
They had her dead and buried.
   Waly O for Roseblush
   Buried under the pine.

She perished as must everyone.
Whom can I blame her death upon?
I should rather
Not involve her father,
Nor did some bumbling fool
Push her into the pool
   Without design;
And we are all far subtler
Than to accuse The Butler.
   Waly O how rotten
   That she was never mine.

Put all the guilt upon the lake
And say she died for drowning's sake.
Call it Nature reflected,
The glass that Love affected,
Or Death's photographer;
The pool that swallowed her,
   One must opine,
Was merely a mirror
Whose image was in error.
   Waly O how falsely
   She died before her time.

Say that she was never brave
But only greedy for the grave;
Say Dongworth's rusty armor
Served only to alarm her.
Then write this of me:
"Were she alive and free,
     With lips like wine,
John Thomas, my English cousin,
Could pluck her like a raisin."
     Waly O for Roseblush
     That she was never mine.

DICK DONGWORTH ON
HIS OWN DEATH

As if he had heard
Of what I've always feared,
Death sent me a minion,
An angel, who inferred
That my own death neared.

With never a doubt
I took him out
And stomped on his bunion
Because of this opinion.

But good my Lord
At our eventual union
Will peel me like an onion
Without a word.
My grief, as He removes my ears
Will reach fruition in His tears.

Let this be heard
Throughout His bright dominion.

For Tellers of Tales

Canzona: A Parting on Shipboard

A bright jeweled beetle like a clump of fire
Glowed at her throat as the sun went rolling out
Over my shoulder, while an incredible
Dark colony of garnets crowning her wrist
Fell, as the deck heaved under us, to shaking.
Our hands touched. The bug blew in the wind and clung,
As if hanged by the nap of the wool she wore.

Could I have found a better jewel to buy her
Than such an insect, it might have made a shout
Of its shining with every crystal syllable
To intimate such farewells from her breast
As if to feign a sorrier forsaking
Than our impermanent parting, as she hung,
Clasped clinging to my neck, and cried and swore.

No lapidary joy of gold and wire
Clasped both our brows so intricately about,
But no mere sea-grief swelled her eyes so full
When I, uneasy lepidopterist,
Made light of the bug; when, as if by my making,
Five crystal tears splashed down her arm among
The garnets, and made them seem pismires all the more.

Their antic sparkling composed our speech entire:
Salt tears flashed within the stones. The sea without
Echoed our silence, till one shrieking gull
Stooped, of a sudden, as if at an amethyst
In the head of the beetle, and all its undertaking
Seemed aimed at that ontic bug; then the bird slung
Its body and its being toward the shore.

O Bug bug bug bug bug that did require
The quietest devotions of our doubt!
At once a lump of crafted mineral,
Whose crystals no reflection could resist,
And a real bettle, whose safety lay in faking
The fixity of jewels, lest some toxin-tongue
Enjoy its Janus facets to the core.

Just then the wind blew up a little higher,
Inflaming the sunset until there was no doubt
But that departure was upon us; still,
The whistle, the irritant bell, had to insist
That the giving of gifts was done, but for our breaking:
A venomous tocsin rolled; when it had rung,
A swarm of June bees drew up in a roar.

No longer then could she and I conspire
About the bug, all bustling and devout,
To make our delaying less discernible.
A pair of antiquarians, we kissed
And clipped, then parted, querulous and quaking.
I wished her joy of the bug, at which she flung
Her jewels to the sea, to spawn upon its floor.

    While in my hand remained five bright tears, wrung
    Like tiny insects of sweat from every pore.

A Word Remembered

All the young poets are writing about the seasons:
It is the summer poor Hippolyte prefers,
While his friend Phoebus despairs of winter's sadness.
The former has become extravagant,
To wallow in languorous tropes, while Phoebus' verses,
Nipped, as if with the cold, get painful and silly.
It was longer ago than I like to think that spring
Fell from their favor and became as dull
As blotters. All of which has made me think
Of the time that Mary was being very pregnant
And would take no beer, but quietly watched us drinking;
Then, mentioning some event of the past April,
She had recourse to name the general season,
But stopped suddenly, as if she had forgotten
A street address she had written down somewhere:

"It happened last—what is it comes before summer?"
And we sat there, not quite believing that this had happened,
Until she finally seemed to have remembered:
"Oh. Yes. Spring." I mention this
Only because we cannot remember now
Who, or what, we felt was being outraged.

For Both of You, the Divorce Being Final

We cannot celebrate with doleful Music
The old, gold panoplies that are so great
To sit and watch; but on the other hand,
To command the nasal krummhorns to be silent,
The *tromba marina* to wail; to have the man
Unlatch the tail gate on his cart, permitting
The sackbut player to extend his crook
And go to work on whimpering divisions;
For us to help prepare the masque itself,
Rigging machinery to collapse the household
Just at the end, rehearsing urchins who
Will trip, all gilded, into the master bedroom
And strip the sheets, is, finally, to confess
That what we lack are rituals adequate
To things like this.
                    We tell some anxious friends
"*Basta!* They know what they are doing"; others
Whom we dislike and who, like queens, betray
Never a trace of uneasiness, we play with:
"No, it could never work, my dears, from the start.
We all knew that. Yes, there's the boy to think of,"
And so on. Everyone makes us nervous. Then,
For a dark instant, as in your unlit foyer
At sundown, bringing a parcel, we see you both
And stifle the awkward question: "What, are *you* here?"
Not because it has been asked before
By Others meeting Underground, but simply
Because we cannot now know which of you
Should answer, or even which of you we asked.
We wait for something to happen in the brown
Shadows around us. Surely there is missing
A tinkle of cymbals to strike up the dirge

And some kind of sounding brass to follow it,
Some hideous and embarrassing gimmick which
Would help us all behave less civilly and
More gently, who mistook civility
So long for lack of gentleness.
                              And since
Weeping's a thing we can no longer manage,
We must needs leave you to the Law's directive:
"You have unmade your bed, now lie about it."
Quickly now: which of you will keep the *Lares,*
Which the *Penates?* And opening the door
We turn like guilty children, mutter something,
And hide in the twilit street.
                              Along the river
The sky is purpling and signs flash out
And on, to beckon the darkness: THE TIME IS NOW . . .
(What time, what time?) Who stops to look in time
Ever, ever? We can do nothing again
For both of you together. And if I burn
An epithalamium six years old to prove
That what we learn is in some way a function
Of what we forget, I know that I should never
Mention it to anyone. When men
Do in the sunny Plaza what they did
Only in dusky corners before, the sunset
Comes as no benison, the assuring license
Of the June night goes unobserved. The lights
Across the river are brighter than the stars;
The water is black and motionless; whatever
Has happened to all of us, it is too late
For something else ever to happen now.

Paysage Moralisé

Astonished poplars hide
Their faces in leafy hands,
Pale green with feigned horror

As, by a fountain's side,
Daphnis misunderstands
Chloe, and makes an error.

Too soon, too soon, he plunges
His hand under the mound
Of taffeta around her!

And so, alas, she flinches,
Leaps up from the ground,
And makes for the grove behind her,

Flinging the old reproach
At lingering Daphnis, who
Had snatched at her only

Because he felt too much
A flatterer, who knew
Of how to praise the lonely.

Under a soupy tree
Mopes Daphnis, joined by all
The brown surrounding landscape:

Even in Arcady
Ego needs must spoil
Such a beautiful friendship!

The Jewels and the Gracchi

Cornelia, with an air
Of amber in her hair,
    Pushed forth her simpering boys
        With a touch of unsureness:
    "These are my jewels and joys.
    Their names are Crystal called;
        It sorts well with their clearness."
    The guests were all appalled

Save one who, with a pair
Of emeralds at her ear,
    Felt for her shining toys
        And nestled to their nearness,
    Making a tiny noise,
    Idolatrous and bald.
        This was unenvying queerness.
    The boys were quite enthralled.

The Fable of the Bears in Winter

I once saw weeping in a wood
The bears that break the heart of God,
When dusty grapes hung from the trees
Revealed themselves as hosts of bees
And rose toward the pale winter sun
(It was most swift and sweetly done!):
They left their nests untenanted,
But had they sallied forth, or fled?
For, standing in a ring below,
All the bears wept to see them go.

Cold winter is a secret season,
Frost and the wind confound the reason,
Perplexing every dying bee;
But it is the bears I weep to see.
When winter and the cold increase
Hiems ursine, shield their peace!
Some shall eat humble beebread, some
Feed on the sumptuous honeycomb;
But none may come to feel or see
Holy sweets in the wintering tree.

For once, to keep a secret from
The bears, less fortunate than some,
God fixed it, with a wild device,
Tight and impressively in ice,
Still shaking feverishly and sunny,
Trapped like a fly in amber honey;

And to protect that shivering dancer
Padlocks were put upon the answer
So that the secrecy was sure;
It was both golden and secure.

Warm bears, with fears as deep as ours,
Can take delight in trees and flowers
And the bees' business, near and far,
And all their gold ambrosia.
But wet bears, with no wits to measure,
Cannot encompass such a treasure
Nor the assumption of the bees
Soft enfold those mysteries:
This final token of belief
Falls to the worst and shiftiest thief.

He trafficks in ridiculous things,
Spots and scraps and wires and strings.
The dark suggestions of the winter
Urge the bad bird to pause and enter:
Let jackdaw, magpie, crane, or jay
Enter then to wrest and prey.
They never let their foul affairs
Breach the deep slumber of the bears,
Who once stood whispering in a ring,
Now warm and innocent till spring.

Each wrapped in a brown indifferent bun,
The Bears! The Bears! Cruelly undone
By birds with eyes so cold and bright
Who come and cheat them in the night.
The Bears! The Bears! Watch how the frost
Leads dreams of golden gifts now lost
Into their anxious hearts, and deep
Among the silver gifts of sleep!
(The while the real adventurer
Succeeds by being bald of fur.)

The sleeping bear is sweet to see.
But look you now how easily
The daw, the jaybird, or the egret
Picks the lock and breaks the Secret.

Enter Machiavel, Waving His Tail

The silly fish deceived him
As he approached the creel:
He thought the whole thing real,
And his black heart believed him.
And so, for a simple meal,
He contrived to creep
Past fisherman asleep.
　　I know it must have peeved him
That I, a sharper angler,
Had acted as his strangler.

I've heard that in all of Europe
The English cats are best,
But had this one guessed
That, smooth as a foreign syrup,
I'd have my wrongs redressed?
Though Italian, I felt ill,
So I hied me off, until
　　I chanced to hear a chirrup.
At the end of the meadow
Waited his beckoning widow.

She was moving at a sparrow
But stopped when I came by
(Triumph in your eye
Shot with a little sorrow
Leaves them far from shy).
I'd hoped she might come
When I killed her Tom;
　　Still, her eyes went narrow
Till she gave me her pardon.
Then we passed into a garden.

Vengeance is seldom easy
For black-like fears remain,
And she thought my pain
Was colicky or crazy.
But courting cats disdain
Kindness from their own:
When she made me sweet moan
    I felt betrayed and lazy,
And thought how the corpse by the river
Would nevermore forgive her.

Living with men has made me
A dialectical cat;
Ergo, I argued that
Her course was to upbraid me:
She refused and she spat
(She claimed no punishment
But held that I'd repent).
    All this was repaid me
When, at the end of the quarrel,
I had her over a barrel.

A Satyre: *Upon the* PHOENIX *and the*
GANDER *in Particular, and upon the Birds in General*

The Argument: The garden keeper is aggrieved to see
how improperly the birds commingle in his garden, how
they abuse singleness and purpose; he bids them be gone
and leave his place to the elements, at which their departure is
envisioned, and song at their going.

Let the birds of wildest birth
  Within my eastern garden's range
  Their myriad pinions arch, and change
These rich blooms for a stranger earth.

The phoenix in the orange phlox
  Shakes the last ashes from his toe:
  Let him with crag-born eagle go
To roost among more fiery rocks.

The zany gander, since gone mute,
  Will scamper toward a finer swill,
  As the mendicant sparrow will
Peck at Hesperidean fruit;

And the black obsequious crow
  Shrieks for some golden bird, his bier,
  Whose feathery bearers soon shall near
That only home of indigo;

The which dark garden of the brine
  Holds deeper burial than this dust:
  Thus phoenix and the gander must
Flee in their several flames from mine.

But doxy dove and cockatoo,
    Bright duchess, tiny sportive queen,
    Compounded in a flush of green,
Have long since burned it into blue;

The thrush, good sister, and the dark
    Reverend mother of the wren
    Together have, with every hen,
Produced that first agreeable spark.

Not long ago the gander broke
    From out his shelly home, his feet
    Gyved with what he could not eat
Of the general parent yolk;

While phoenix made rejection
    Of his first ashes, sent to dust:
    Now both these birds have come to lust
In single flight, inaction.

At this expense of wasted flame,
    Like tropic duchess and her dove
    Shall phoenix with the gander move,
Cock by cock, as dame with dame.

Strangely conjoint, the dames abash
    Mutual union, and the cocks
    Like separate blossoms of the phlox
Mock unity in mounds of ash.

If these bad marriages must be:
    One sundered; common difference;
    Let the partners pass from hence,
Part, and be wedded in the sea.

Perches that once were trees and rocks
   Are stone and water, smoke and wood;
   The mud in which the gander stood
Choirs with once-consuming phlox;

Pink embers of the phlox undone,
   The mud's last heritage of dust,
   To the wind's company shall trust
This proper prothalamion:

PROTHALAMION

ASHES: Parthenia of Unity
         By each bird beneath the sea
         Upon one bed shall ravished be.

DUST: Never let a feather falter
         Till, upon that coral altar,
         Each singed wing may smack the psalter.

ASHES: Mother of all gardens, mate
         These mad birds, while inviolate,
         Ashes keep the last estate.

DUST: Anemones, conjoin to finger
         All the parts of every singer;
         Let them not kneel too long, nor linger.

BOTH: Let them, each by each, be led
         As, down to general sand, the dead,
         To come to Unity in bed.

Late August on the Lido

To lie on these beaches for another summer
Would not become them at all,
And yet the water and her sands will suffer
When, in the fall,
These golden children will be taken from her.

It is not the gold they bring: enough of that
Has shone in the water for ages
And in the bright theater of Venice at their backs;
But the final stages
Of all those afternoons when they played and sat

And waited for a beckoning wind to blow them
Back over the water again
Are scenes most necessary to this ocean.
What actors then
Will play when these disperse from the sand below them?

All this is over until, perhaps, next spring;
This last afternoon must be pleasing.
Europe, Europe is over, but they lie here still,
While the wind, increasing,
Sands teeth, sands eyes, sands taste, sands everything.

Heat of Snow

Anne par jeu me jecta de la neige

CLÉMENT MAROT

When she, laughing, plastered a snowball on me,
all the crisp, white, sherbety cold we both were
waiting for seemed suddenly to have melted;
                    somehow, her shoulders

fell against my own as the thing hit both of
us at once, and then as we fell together
on the high, soft drift that the sun made bright we
                    burned, oh we burned, but

not because such sunlight was any warmer
than the glaring ice on the pond beyond us,
forcing us to squint as we sat and shivered
                    later together

when we thought how even inside the snow there
blazed such warmth; how nothing was colder now than
our informing flame; and, if ice perhaps might
                    cool it a little,

then how painful, blinding, the prospect toward the
shimmering pond where, lifeless, the ice awaited
first our shielded gaze, then our tired march and
                    final arrival.

For Certain Others

Autumn in Another State

It is in low silence, always, that one errs,
Hearing the trees outside distinctly, where
The high wind, generally, obscures and blurs

The most discrete intentions, and defers
The private mumming that harms beyond repair.
It is in low silence, always, that one errs.

Night sounds in ponds, disturbances in firs,
Suggest that beyond the window, in the air,
The high wind generally obscures and blurs.

Thus all his whispers disappear in hers:
When the humming of touch alone has laid her bare,
It is in low silence always that one errs.

He finds that when morning weather disinters
Buried decisions, his eyes can't stand the glare;
The high wind generally obscures and blurs.

Forget him. Observe the erasure that occurs
When, after actions emerge as seeming clear
(It is in low silence, always, that one errs),
The high wind generally obscures, and blurs.

Winter in Indiana

FOR J. M. ZITO

With March the snow has no undue extension;
To stamp, then, across patches of footpath,
Sodden, and below the recent drenching
Parched by the windy intervals of no snow,
Is to remain free of any sense of expanse
Or any remembrance of stretches of anything.

In January almost anything
Can hold, for a moment, the appearance of extension
Beyond the bounds of its own white expanse;
And to know that beneath lies the familiar footpath
Can be either wonderful or dull, like snow,
Deep and unspoiled by anything like a drenching.

But in late, rainy winters, grayed by drenching,
Incessant, and unbounded by anything,
No January and no flat, white snow
Make the horizon real, or, by extension,
Can give one any sense of an end to the footpath
Deep in the simple direction of its expanse.

Visitors come, impressed by the snow's expanse,
But tell us quite frankly that it needs a drenching:
"Great," they say, "but one can't see the footpath,"
Then hurry off, with a fear of anything
That looks, toward evening, like this false extension,
These purpling shadows at the edge of snow.

Our own fear is that the truth about the snow
Can only be stated in terms of its expanse,
That all that's real is the idea of extension;

Then loves and attachments thaw, and turn to drenching
White fields of Hope with wet, gray Anything
No matter though we wander or keep to the footpath.

No matter, either, if we who dwell on the footpath
With the simple love we squander on the snow
Made prayers that really amounted to anything,
Though they were "Father, send us a sense of expanse"
Or, rather, "Father, send us a definite drenching
To end all this difficult, tenuous, white extension."

For, drenching and darkening withal, the snow
Loses expanse when one first discerns the footpath
Whose own extension may move toward anything.

Science and Human Behavior

FOR B. F. SKINNER

Feeling that it is vaguely undignified
To win someone else's bet for him by choosing
The quiet girl in the corner, not refusing
But simply not preferring the other one;
Abashed by having it known that we decide
To save the icing on the chocolate bun
Until the last, that we prefer to ride
Next to the window always; more than afraid
Of knowing that They know what sends us screaming
Out of the movie; even shocked by the dreaming
Our friends do about us, we vainly hope
That certain predictions never can be made,
That the mind can never spin the Golden Rope
By which we feel bound, determined, and betrayed;

But rather, if such a thing exists at all,
Three nasty Thingummies should hold it, twisting
Strand onto endless strand, always resisting
Our own old impulse to pull the string and see
Just what would happen, or to feel the small
But tingling tug upon the line, to free
The captives so that we might watch them crawl
Back into deeper water again. It is well
To leave such matters in their power, trusting
To the blasé discretion of disgusting
Things like the Two who spin and measure, and
The Third and surely The Most Horrible,
Whom we'd best forget, within whose bony hand
Lies crumpled the Secret she will never tell.

Which Secret concerns the nature of the string
That all Three tend, and whether it be the wire
Designed to receive the message or to fire
The tiny initial relay. In the end,
The question is whether merely Determining
Or really Knowing is what we most pretend
To honor because it seems most frightening
Or worship because we hold it most to blame.
I once saw Dr. Johnson in a vision;
His hat was in his hand, and a decision
Of import on his lips. "Our will," he said,
"Is free, and there's an end on't." All the same,
Atropos and her sisters, overhead,
Grinned at this invocation of their name.

Jefferson Valley

The tops of the spruces here have always done
Ragged things to the skies arranged behind them
Like slates at twilight; and the morning sun
Has marked out trees and hedgerows, and defined them
In various greens, until, toward night, they blur
Back into one rough palisade again,
Furred thick with dusk. No wind we know can stir
This olive blackness that surrounds us when
It becomes the boundary of what we know
By limiting the edge of what we see.
When sunlight shows several spruces in a row,
To know the green of a particular tree
        Means disbelief in darkness; and the lack
        Of a singular green is what we mean by black.

Overcast

Bare alder and twiggy locust on our hill
Scumble about a steep track by the fence
That ends in ruined pasture, cold and still.
Often up here the false grey light invents
Astonishing grey pastures, to betray
Even our most primitive ways of knowing
One branch from the sky behind it, or a spray
Of yarrow from the rocky outcrop growing
Behind it. Seasons too destroy the real
Distinctions between what things appear to be.
Is stripping this hilltop, though, of grey to peel
From the trees their appearance of identity,
  Or to show that what we feel is, after all,
  Most real because it is most general?

A Theory of Waves

Having no surface of its own, the pond,
Under the shifting grey contingency
Of morning mists, extends even beyond
The swamp beside it, until presently
The thinning air declares itself to be
No longer water, and the pond itself
Is still for a moment, and no longer air.
Then waking bass glide from their sandy shelf,
And sets of concentric circles everywhere
Expand through some imaginary thing
Whose existence must be assumed, until they meet,
When incorporeal ripples, ring on ring,
Disturb a real surface, as if, with dripping feet,
Some dark hypothesis had made retreat.

A Theory of Measure

We draw our own dimensions; after all
The yardsticks are outlawed, still, in secrecy,
Our shadows at evening tell us that we're tall;

We know that hours ripen, drop, and fall
Without a clock to pluck them hurriedly.
We draw our own dimensions, after all,

Almost as frantically. It may appall
Us that we are much older when we see
Our shadows at evening; tell us that we're tall,

And we wonder what in us you think is small,
Remembering doodles that sometimes, nervously,
We draw (our own dimensions, after all,

May be asserted somewhere in the scrawl).
That we are shorter than our poplar tree
Our shadows at evening tell us. That we're tall

The fifteen-year-old marks upon the wall,
Our shorter friends, both show us constantly.
We draw our own dimensions, after all
Our shadows at evening tell us that we're tall.

The Fear of Trembling

FOR GEORGE KATEB

If it is true that we no longer seek
To avoid the three peculiar trees that grow
At the edge of the wood, it is because we know
That even the wood itself can hold no terrors.
If, without fear of falling, we can speak
Three times of the devil, ignore the fatal errors
Of leaving nail parings and bits of hair about,
Or even our impress in wrinkles on a sheet,
It is because of too many occasions
On which the devil never appears. And suasions
That spiky crones have urged on images
Crudely depicting us too often meet
With scorn, or any of the various stages
Of nonchalance, and are put down, without

Any benefit of dramaturgy
By which to frighten the old bitches back
(To make white magic is to believe in black.)
And we have lost the less accessible fear
Of pushing past seers, and the sober clergy
Of the God in his normal forms, crossing the blear
Ravines and craggy slopes to come upon
The cave of the Wolf-Zeus, where the blinding sun
Beats on the rocky wall, but where we cast
No shadow. For, likewise, when our last
Guests have departed, and the night's debris
Grows pale at dawn, the Uninvited one
Whose name we could not remember turns out to be
Someone with an identity all his own

And no real *Doppelgänger* after all.
Thus, as we lose our terror of the night,
The Sun God's Sadducees are put to flight,
Dispersing underground and carrying
The relics of Certainty with them, as a pall
Of unreal darkness blurs their exiting.
Their sun sets and our sky grows colder: we
Are left in that hard-rock desert, bare of tree
And stripped of mirage, that Locke looked out and saw
Under the setting sunlight, faint and raw;
All the sure horrors have vanished from a world
Bathed in the twilight of Probability
That sent the heebie-jeebies down and hurled
Them, screaming, into the fringes of mystery,

The margins of truth. Well then, we have got
Our landscape plain enough now, and the rope
Of Illusion, hung in front of us like Hope,
Has been withdrawn. But, peering across the sand,
We are unaccustomed to so much nothing. What,
Then, if we tremble a little? To understand
Exactly what it means to shiver, when
We have grown used to the chilly air, is, then,
Perhaps to know that our knowledge of what is true
Of the world casts doubt on what we thought we knew
About ourselves, or at least on how it was
We came to know it. And when other men
With other minds stare at our hands, it is
Because theirs tremble too, and only in

Such signs and portents do we know our fear
To lie. For only in the fear of trembling,
When all the physical specters disappear,
Are the unknowable present dangers clear:
Watch how we shake! We cannot be dissembling,
We cannot be deceived; something resembling
Something frightening, even now, is here.

The Sundial

horas tempestatis quoque enumero

FOR ELENA LEVIN

When in the festival of August heat
The air stops throbbing over the balustrades
Bordering the terrazzo, and for a moment
The white pilasters on the Older Wing,
No longer mixed with the rough pink of the wall,
Regain the cold demeanor of their marble,
A second of stillness halts the processional
Of hours on the heels of hotter hours
Winding their turn and counterturn and stand,
While the great concrete lions on the steps
Seem always at the moment of fidgeting
And the house cats are no less motionless,
Their tails on the verge of twitching, never now, but
    Always the following second.

Then servants clamor for the city. Rifts
In the masonry appear to be much wider
Than we had ever thought them, tufts of grass
Thrust out through the cracked base of the sundial
And wilting morning-glory menaces
Its bronzed ingenuous face with blurring shadows:
Only then can we feel the sudden storm
To be overdue for the fraction of an instant,
For the dark wind is upon us then, the heat
Fractures like concrete, mirrored in the sky
By the thinnest of cracks across the clouds and followed
By the expectedly delayed report
That is always graver than we care to think,
    Rumbling out of the darkness.

Then both the sundial and the birdbath run
Over into the lawn, and bubbling puddles
Drip down the steps. Neglected by a wall,
Two marble *putti* weep as they are bathed,
Still leering through the rusty stains about
Their mouths. The ruin and the summerhouse
Are empty, but through the trumpeting downpour, some-
    where,
Inside long windows, Leopoldine is playing
Her *Gradus ad Parnassum,* while nearby
A Chinese philosopher on a silk screen shrinks
From the thunder he has always held to be
The ultimate disorder, as the wind
Wrinkles a painted heron on the bank
    Barely suggested behind him.

The hour of storm goes by unmarked; but when
The lowering sun hangs over the afternoon,
Making gold veins in all the marble again,
Revealing crystals in the carpeted lawns,
When the air is clear and cool with a new stillness,
The girls emerge from the house with laughter and teacups
(The youngest stands on a swing in the oldest elm
Facing her visitor from the City, who
Is tall and thin in black clothes, and they swing
Back and forth like a slow clock); only then
Does the cool shadow on the sundial show
The elapsed time of a distant age, the drip
Of water from its sharp, ostensive finger
Still falling at ever slower intervals,
    Dropping (the swing slowing), dropping.

I cannot but wonder what you meant last month
When, recounting for us an old hour of storm,
You invoked implausible landscapes, as you said:
"We had a quarrel once, and after the quarrel

He left, and I went home and wept; and then,
Still weeping, I played ping-pong with my sisters . . ."
And your weeping echoed from another Europe
Of houses to which we would never be invited,
The girls in long, white dresses and the game
Disconsolate enough to last an hour
While the storm raged on outside the draperies,
Spattering the terrace; while the sundial
Said nothing, remembering everything, as the rain
        Slowly eroded its features.

When such heat sends us fleeing from the city,
Pursues, and then gives up its chase, the thunder
Blows the retreating blasts and leaves us then
Stranded in another time, outside
Some city—Dublin or St. Petersburg,
Salzburg or Prague—with no trains, and the roads
Impassably muddy; and we are confronted
With our own dream entire, with the side
Of the image we never see: the sundial in darkness
Or cracked from its base and lying in one of the cellars,
Numbering storm-tossed hours but telling nothing,
Until, before the image dissolves, we can see
The marble house, the park, the filmy girls
        Standing and swinging in silence;
The unambiguous shadow on the sundial
Cast by the last glance of departing sunlight,
        Measuring always this moment.

The Observatory

How vainly open eyes amaze
Themselves with the synoptic gaze!
And cloud the mediant air between
The image and the object seen,
Whose public face may never ask
The one behind it to unmask.
Better to see, I made my home
This dark eye, a transparent dome.

To pierce with pools of mental light
The pudency that shades the night,
I turn my stare on hidden suns,
Forbidden constellations,
Each planet spinning in her niche,
And bright elliptic visions which
No intervening prospect mars:
The winking habits of the stars.

Thus I, crazy astronomer,
Whose heavens are this earth, confer
Among my lenses with the few
Who sought for the forbidden view:
Sweet Insight's Martyrs! each displays
The Keyhole, emblem of his praise,
Unlocked by only those who try
The fitting key, the peering eye.

Where Privacy was put to rout
Actaeon peeped true beauty out;
Lot's wife risked all that she might know
What salt had lost its savor so;
Tom's blind eyes clasped, without remorse,

Chaste whiteness straddled on a horse,
And *Orpheus* turned about to see
His noumenal *Eurydice*.

Ah, what a life with them I led!
Bright data danced inside my head;
By brambles, where I used to lie,
Endangering the naked eye,
I sped my floating sight to drift
Round *Sandra* standing in her shift,
To seize a patch of pink and white
Undifferentiated light:

My mother's opera glass laid bare
The sensibilia lurking there
(Sharp images that should have kept
Secret the Things in which they slept),
Like crystal thoughts that hidden dwell
Within the gem's deceptive shell,
Or mild affections, unbetrayed
By the dark face of a dark shade.

Such innocency as was mine
When, clinging to my neighbor's vine,
I learned that all but blinding lies
Are interdicted from the eyes,
Infused our former State, where turned
Two heavenly bodies; as each burned
The other took his light therefrom:
A perfect Planetarium!

The Beautiful, the virtuous Mean
Were then permitted to be seen
Before false, opened eyes effaced
Those bright inscriptions with distaste;
And letters which enclosed the True
By clothes were folded out of view,

Whose blind impress upon the seal
Made the apparent the unreal.

I, in my glassy Paradise,
With fading sight anatomize
The figures of the world, and trope,
As rod and staff, my telescope,
Awaiting the descent of night
When I shall read the darkened light
Behind day's unperceiving pall;
While seeing nothing, knowing all.

From *Peeping Tom*

By the Sea

Joe, mach die Musik von damals nach!

The dark, gray receding tide uncovers
New reaches of white sand; and underfoot
Dry bony driftwood moves into the shade,
    Growing as cold as
    The sparrow-colored
Cliffs that hover above the beach to mark
The rooted boundaries beyond all which
Nothing made of the sea may pass. The flying
    Onshore winds only
    Flap through an awning

Over the empty beach house. The sun becomes
Paler than one could believe. The treachery
Of memory is probably no deeper now
    Than it is ever;
    But when, toward evening,
Summer shivers into covering darkness,
Spreading no particular season's chill
Down the beach, older remembered images
    Invade the prospect.
    Like the preposterous

Youngsters who come prancing over the sand,
Waiting for sundown on the hard, cold beach
To send them groping for each other's furry
    Parts, in the blackness
    Of sandy blankets,
Handling the loneliness, the only *Angst*
Each has ever known, in the only ways
Occurring to them, we ourselves expend
    Passion on peeping
    (At seascapes, perhaps)

Or on grabbing a feel of this night air
Nearly as nervously as they. Their rubbish,
Found, at morning, in pools among the rocks
    Manages somehow
    To hold a simple
Bare innocence always (white, floating relics
Of hurried ceremonies, looking fairly
Like the dead blowfish that meander round them)
    Remaining harmless;
    While all the horrid

Nonsense of moments we have left behind
Drifts up onto the shores of consciousness
And waits to betray us. Even this stark scene
    Robbed of its being
    By other beaches,
Winds, sunsets, tides, our own touches of darkness,
Senseless, gauche, and inconsiderate gifts
Given us by what once we were, and baited
    With what, in all traps,
    Seems most attractive,

Even this strange new beach becomes, beclouded
By unforgetting eyes, one of the Good
Old Places. And the roaring of the sand's edge,
    Tunditur unda,
    Thundering under
High, loud breakers blasting the uneven
Tides of silence, alternating with windy
Pianissimi that whimper through the cold,
    Sighing to cadence,
    Is quickly cuddled

By pampering recollection, in whose embrace
All the wild music is drowned in the Old Song
With the embarrassing title that is lodged
    Deep in our hearing.
    All its heaving,

Precious, banal progressions work toward damping
Everything that purports to be musical.
The stodgiest tune will have its aftermath
    (When once forgotten,
    Or, like the gods of

A place one has been banished from, remembered
In all despite of better judgment) always
Remaining, like the flapping of the wind,
    Tumbling of breakers,
    The gray terns' braying,
Somehow prior to other singing. Faced
With waves, surrounded by sand, tangled in tall
Bundles of crab grass, we are marooned in strains
    And chords of habit
    Because of having

Faced other beaches, if only remembered
Faintly as being dreamt of, mediating
Between us and the scene before us, fading
    Softly to darkness.

The Great Bear

Even on clear nights, lead the most supple children
Out onto hilltops, and by no means will
They make it out. Neither the gruff round image
From a remembered page nor the uncertain
Finger tracing that image out can manage
To mark the lines of what ought to be there,
Passing through certain bounding stars, until
The whole massive expanse of bear appear
Swinging, across the ecliptic; and, although
The littlest ones say nothing, others respond,
Making us thankful in varying degrees
For what we would have shown them: "There it is!"
"I see it now!" Even "Very like a bear!"
Would make us grateful. Because there is no bear

We blame our memory of the picture: trudging
Up the dark, starlit path, stooping to clutch
An anxious hand, perhaps the outline faded
Then; perhaps could we have retained the thing
In mind ourselves, with it we might have staged
Something convincing. We easily forget
The huge, clear, homely dipper that is such
An event to reckon with, an object set
Across the space the bear should occupy;
But even so, the trouble lies in pointing
At any stars. For one's own finger aims
Always elsewhere: the man beside one seems
Never to get the point. "No! The bright star
Just above my fingertip." The star,

If any, that he sees beyond one's finger
Will never be the intended one. To bring

Another's eye to bear in such a fashion
On any single star seems to require
Something very like a constellation
That both habitually see at night;
Not in the stars themselves, but in among
Their scatter, perhaps, some old familiar sight
Is always there to take a bearing from.
And if the smallest child of all should cry
Out on the wet, black grass because he sees
Nothing but stars, though claiming that there is
Some bear not there that frightens him, we need
Only reflect that we ourselves have need

Of what is fearful (being really nothing)
With which to find our way about the path
That leads back down the hill again, and with
Which to enable the older children standing
By us to follow what we mean by "This
Star," "That one," or "The other one beyond it."
But what of the tiny, scared ones?—Such a bear,
Who needs it? We can still make do with both
The dipper that we always knew was there
And the bright, simple shapes that suddenly
Emerge on certain nights. To understand
The signs that stars compose, we need depend
Only on stars that are entirely there
And the apparent space between them. There

Never need be lines between them, puzzling
Our sense of what is what. What a star does
Is never to surprise us as it covers
The center of its patch of darkness, sparkling
Always, a point in one of many figures.
One solitary star would be quite useless,
A frigid conjecture, true but trifling;
And any single sign is meaningless

If unnecessary. Crab, bull, and ram,
Or frosty, irregular polygons of our own
Devising, or finally the Great Dark Bear
That we can never quite believe is there—
Having the others, any one of them
Can be dispensed with. The bear, of all of them,

Is somehow most like any one, taken
At random, in that we always tend to say
That just because it might be there; because
Some Ancients really traced it out, a broken
And complicated line, webbing bright stars
And fainter ones together; because a bear
Habitually appeared—then even by day
It is for us a thing that should be there.
We should not want to train ourselves to see it.
The world is everything that happens to
Be true. The stars at night seem to suggest
The shapes of what might be. If it were best,
Even, to have it there (such a great bear!
All hung with stars!), there still would be no bear.

THE YALE SERIES OF YOUNGER POETS, *which is designed to provide a publishing medium for the first volumes of promising poets, is open to men and women under forty who have not previously had a book of verse published. W. H. Auden, the Editor of the Series, selects the winning volume in the annual contest and writes a preface for it. Manuscripts should be received before March 1 and should be addressed to the Editor, Yale Series of Younger Poets, Yale University Press, New Haven, Connecticut. Rules of the contest will be sent upon request.*

VOLUMES 41, 46–50, 52–54 ARE IN PRINT.